Textured Skin II

Affects & Effects of A Burn Survivor

Elizabeth Grey

ISBN: 978-0-578-76737-6 (print)
ISBN: 978-0-578-81205-2 (e book)

Publisher:
Tressie's Tales
PO Box 388
Libby, MT 59923

Editor: Melinda Gholson

Photography
Front cover, back cover, and "about author" photos by
http://www.jessicalynnephotography.com

DEDICATION

This book is dedicated to my parents,

Cary and Elizabeth,

for their never ending support of any project I might decide to pursue. They are two of the bravest people I know who have persevered through many hardships in their lives, often times against incredible odds! Their encouragement and strength of character has been a shining example for both myself and my sister. Always willing to share any good fortune they might receive, my parents attempted to do their part to make the world a happier place, one act of kindness at a time.
Giving me their blessing to share the events that resulted from such a tragic day so long ago demonstrates yet another way these two individuals are committed to contributing to bringing hope to those who feel hopeless.

FOREWORD

by

Melinda Roseberry Gholson

Elizabeth Grey is my first cousin and my grandparents' favorite grandchild. She is the favorite for two reasons. First, her childhood musical talent allowed her to become church pianist at Riverside Baptist Church in Mobile, Alabama. (Riverside was my grandparents' sacred worship place.) Second, Elizabeth experienced a life-threatening burn as a pre-schooler. All the anxiety, stress, and fear related to a childhood illness created a powerful bond with those who prayed and cared for her during her recuperation. She mercifully has no memory of the tragedy. However, she bears a scar which has become a badge of honor for her and a help to her patients. Her story has given numerous patients and their families hope.

ACKNOWLEDGMENTS

This section is one of the hardest to compose because the individuals that provided input and encouragement to me cannot be recognized enough by a few words of praise. However, I hope the mention of just a few of the ways they kept me going on this endeavor will convey at least a portion of my gratitude.

Joy Carlson was one of the first people to read the initial draft and was instrumental in keeping the personal feel of the story line. She felt it crucial that it remain as if she were sitting on the couch with me listening to me tell the story. Also, her proof reading skills have been valuable in keeping the typos to a minimum.

Fran Francis advised the addition of more cases that would illustrate my interaction with patients. Also, both Fran and Melinda encouraged the addition of photos.

Melinda Gholson is responsible for the final product you will read on these pages. She has been an editor for years and has a keen sense for wording that is clear and concise, but remains with the general feel of the story.

CONTENTS

INTRODUCTION

From Me to You

The adventures described in the following pages are stories about my life as a burn victim and my career as a practicing physical therapist treating patients.   These recollections are meant as commentary from the viewpoint of someone who has been on both sides of the patient/therapist relationship. These memories are not meant to serve as documentation of these events. They result from a perspective developed, over time, about a population with unique characteristics and needs. By telling these events, I hope the reader will finish this book with more insight into the situations burn victims face.

The duties of a physical therapist can be tedious. I have spared the reader most of these technical details except where necessary for context. The cases discussed are a small portion of the patient population I treated as a physical therapist.

Throughout my physical therapy career, I have encountered patients of all ages and from all walks of life - from the very young to the very old. When sharing the details of my own childhood accident with other burn patients, I realized that I could make a difference in their psychological healing.

My narrative begins with my childhood accident, which has affected how I live and work. Looking back on my life I am reminded how really blessed I have been. From a loving and supportive family to a fulfilling and rewarding career, my journey, so far, has resulted in a life of positive outcomes.

Because my burn accident occurred at such a young age, I have no memory of it. Therefore, my story combines different accounts told to me throughout my life. It is worth noting that my parents did not discuss the details of my accident with me until I graduated from physical therapy school and took a job in a burn unit. Until this time, what I knew of my accident was what other family members had told me. As my parents told me their account of how I was burned, it was obvious they could hardly hold back the tears. Since that initial conversation, my parents have gradually revealed more details to me. I have been spared the emotional pain they experienced because I have no memory of those days.

Before I began writing this book, my parents and I never discussed the treatments I performed on burn patients or the fact that I had shared my story with some of my patients. I don't think it makes the memories of my accident any easier for my parents to bear, but maybe they can see that some purpose did come from the horrible ordeal.

CHAPTER 1

Background

It was mid-December, 1964, in a small town in southern Alabama. The Christmas spirit was creating it's usual excitement and anxiety which influences both our attitudes and actions this time of year. The joy of the season was almost consumed by the holiday rush that was taking over nearly every household and business in the community. As you strolled down the avenues the anticipation of the season was palpable all around.

The town streets were lit up with colorful Christmas decorations welcoming all the shoppers. Merchants decorated their store fronts demonstrating their holiday spirit in attempts to lure customers into their shops.   Churches announced their yearly programs for praise and worship. Community billboards advertised the town's Christmas parade.

Neighborhoods held decorating contests to encourage everyone to display their holiday spirit. From the tacky to the elaborate, you could ride the streets in the evening and enjoy all the excitement of Christmas. It seemed everyone was preparing for participation in family dinners, religious ceremonies, and community events. Christmas cheer was on full display!

Even though our house was located outside the city limits along US Highway 31, we participated in the display of Christmas decorations like city slickers. Since Thanksgiving Day Mom had filled the house with lots of seasonal cheer by placing plenty of lights and ornaments on the Christmas tree, hanging a wreath on the front door, and placing holiday arrangements strategically throughout the house. Dad even got in on the action by hanging lights on the outside of the house.

As a child, Christmas celebrations had always seemed magical from the secretive visit by Santa Claus on Christmas morning to the salvation that the birth of the baby Jesus represents for Christians. As adults, however, planning and executing all these wonderful celebrations can mean more stress than relaxation. We all want the holidays to be joyful and most of us go above and beyond to make this a reality:

- We rush to get the shopping done before all the things we want to buy are sold.
- We frantically wrap the gifts with the perfect bow.
- We can't forget the baking! Everyone has their favorite holiday pie, cookie, or cake.

Mom and dad had an extra reason to celebrate this particular year. After two years of marriage my parents had been able to build a new house and had moved into the 3 bedroom one bath country home just 6 months earlier. Being a stay-at-home mom at the time, my mother had been able to oversee a lot of the construction details. Her father was the general contractor, so she was able to give input on many of the structural designs. Decorating their house for the holidays gave them the opportunity to highlight their American dream coming true - owning their home.

My parents were hardworking, church going people who often struggled to make ends meet. However, this was a time in their lives they thought financially things might actually be unfolding as they had planned. After completing his training at trade school, Dad had a good job as a linotype operator at the local newspaper. Mom would be starting a new job soon which would provide some extra income. Now, life was better for both of them as adults compared to their family struggles growing up and they were thankful for what they had.

Dad spent most of his childhood and adolescent years in southern Mississippi being educated in a one room school house for grades 1-12. His parents were poor farmers who struggled to simply provide enough food to keep the family fed much less have any money left over for extras at Christmas time. At the age of 15 his family moved to Mobile, Alabama, where he was suddenly thrown into a high school experience with around 1,000 students in one grade! The family farm was sold for the chance to get a fresh start as a gas station owner in the big city. Even with the big city influence, religious activities remained the center of their lives.

Mom was also from a small town in Mississippi's neighbor state of Alabama. She moved to Mobile, Alabama, at the age of 10. Her parents were also looking for a fresh start in one of the many job opportunities in the big city. However, any financial achievement was quickly consumed in alcohol by my grandfather, making extra cash for Christmas gifts almost nonexistent. Religious activities were introduced to my mother by her grandmother and grandfather who helped stabilize her life.

After meeting at church, they began dating and eventually married in the same Baptist church. Although from slightly different backgrounds, they managed to find common ground on which to build a relationship with one another. When dad's short military career was over, they migrated back to the small town atmosphere in an attempt to have a quiet, peaceful life together and raise a family.

At this time, I was an only child, so mom and dad were relatively new to the parenting scene and still adjusting to the energy level of a toddler. I was almost 16 months old with the curiosity of a cat. (Mother tells me that growing up I was the child who got into everything requiring her to watch me with more frequency than my sibling.) One evening in December, 1964, would prove to be no exception. My curiosity would quite literally almost cost me my life and the sanity of my parents. The events of this night and the situations it presented years later would come to guide the course of my life in ways neither I, nor my parents, could ever have imagined.

CHAPTER 2

The Accident

In 1964, family dinners were a common and expected event in American society, especially in the south. The housewives usually prepared the meals to be served when the working husband got home from his job. Our household was no different than this stereotype of American families. One evening in December our peaceful family dinner would be post-poned by an ordeal that would change the lives of everyone involved.

After a long day on the printing press at the local newspaper, Dad was in the den relaxing in his recliner and watching the evening news.   Mean-while, mom was in the kitchen preparing the evening meal filling the house with mouth watering aromas. As I played with my toys on the den floor, pots and pans rattling creating the background noise for the current events and weather being reported on one of three TV stations. By the way, only one TV per household!   So, the parents usually chose the sta-tion which would provide the entertainment for the night.

In the final steps of the meal prep process, mom poured boiling water over the tea bags to brew some sweet tea, a favorite of most southern folks. As usual, she let the strings on the tea bags hang over the edge of the pot while the brewing complet-ed.

Concentrating on the completion of dinner preparation, mom was not aware that I had entered the kitchen. She thought I was in the den with Dad being entertained by a toy box full of things designed to keep me occupied for hours. However, like all children at this age I was more interested in helping mom in the kitchen than tinkering with any toy.

As I wandered into the kitchen I spotted the pot with the tea bag tags hanging over the edge. The gentle side-to-side sway of the tags of the tea bags as they hung over the side of the pot was tranquilizing. The rhythm made them irresistible! I just had to find out what was inside.

On my tip toes with my right hand I reached up, grabbed the tags, and pulled them toward me. The entire pot of brewing tea came splashing down on me! As the scalding hot water hit the bend of my right arm it splattered all over my face and upper body. The only thing between the water and my skin was the sweater I was wearing.

Blood curdling screams rang throughout the house as I was alerting the world of my pain! My mother turned in horror from her cooking station at the stove to see steam billowing off my right arm, face, and portions of my abdomen. Seconds later, Dad rushed into the kitchen to see what was so upsetting to his little girl.

For a few moments, my parents were in a state of shock! How could this happen? Dad did not see me leave the den! Mom did not see me enter the kitchen!

How could they have been so distracted to be un-aware of my actions? No time for those doubts at this moment, though. There would be plenty of time for reflection in the days, weeks, months, and even years ahead.

Franticly, they tried to decide the best course of action. At that time, conflicting theories about whether or not to remove clothes that were over burns as well as whether or not to pour cold water on burns made the decision even more difficult. Also, the severity of the injury was not immediately evident. The water that splashed on my face created only superficial burns which did not blister until later. The majority of the scalding water was trapped un-der the clothing I was wearing which camouflaged the fact that the heat from the water was being held around my arm creating a "baking" effect!

They were not sure what to do next - go to the emergency room or call the family doctor? Who should they contact for advice? Both sets of grand-parents lived over an hour away, so why upset them unnecessarily until they knew how severe the injury? Quick discussion resulted in deciding to not remove my clothes.

Living several miles from the nearest town, they called a neighbor who lived a few hundred yards away. He rushed to the house and found two very distraught young parents and a severely burned toddler. As I screamed in pain, he immediately drove (raced, according to other accounts of the story) all of us to the closest emergency room. This 5-10 minute ride to the small, rural hospital must have seemed like an eternity with a screaming child in the car. (Although, this was just the beginning of what would seem like time passing at a snail's pace . The stages of care that were about to unfold for my parents would be a nightmare they could not have imagined.)

Upon arrival in the emergency room the staff attended to my burns relatively promptly. After the nurses on duty at the emergency room bandaged my arm, I was admitted to the hospital. However, no physician had examined my wounds and my parents were told the doctor on call would be in later. My grandparents arrived a short time later to help comfort my parents and assist in attempts to console me. We all settled in for what would be the first of many sleepless nights in a hospital room.

As the sun rose the next morning, still no doctor had been into my room to examine my wounds. Morning turned into afternoon and then the next evening rolled around without a physician to check on my burns. After 24 hours in the hospital, no nurse or staff member had changed my bandages or even looked at my burns to determine the status. My parents had been unable to get me to eat or drink anything since the accident. My entire family was concerned. My condition seemed to be getting worse and still no physician had examined me.

Listening to their child moan in pain all night was taking it's toll on my parents' mental state. They had had the entire evening to contemplate the events leading up to the accident. Dad wondered, "what on the evening news had been so important that it distracted me long enough not to notice my daughter's absence? How could I not realize she was not with her toys?" Mom wondered, "why could I not hear her climbing on the counter at least in time to stop the pot from completely soaking her clothes!" Was the TV too loud? Were the pots and pans too close to the edge of the counter? Their guilt feelings over the situation were compounded by the fact that the hospital they had chosen to care for their daughter had essentially done nothing more than bandage the wounds.

Now, 36 hours had elapsed since being admitted to the hospital. My parents were watching their second sunset from my hospital room and still no physician had examined my me. I was still not eating or drinking anything. All I did was cry! Totally frustrated with the care I was receiving, my parents contacted our primary care physician and informed him of the incident.   After consultation with our family doctor, my parents picked me up in their arms and carried me out of the hospital. They put me in their car and personally transported me to another hospital in Mobile, Alabama, where the family doctor had called ahead and told the emergency room physicians to expect us.

It was a 45 minute drive to the hospital in Mobile, Alabama, and during the transport my mother became even more worried when I stopped crying and she had trouble keeping me conscious. I can only imagine the level of tension in the car as my dad drove like he was in a NASCAR race while my mother yelled "faster" for what would probably be the only time in their 50+ year marriage she encouraged him to speed!

The doctors at the Mobile hospital immediately began wound care the minute my parents brought me through the emergency room doors!   Dad carried me into the treatment room where the doctors removed the bandages. My Dad almost passed out from the gangrenous smell being emitted! The general consensus was that if my parents had not acted when they did by taking me to another hospital, I probably would have died from the infection.   Even for 1964 standards, the doctors and staff considered the medical treatment I had received initially to be substandard at best!

Being in the medical field, I can't fathom the type of neglect that occurred at the hospital my parents initially took me for treatment. The staff surely had knowledge of the pain and discomfort I was suffering as evidenced by my constant crying. Maybe they were not properly trained to deal with pediatric cases and their fear of further harming me by doing the wrong thing kept them from attempting to do anything. Hopefully, in hind sight, the lack of procedures and mind set of the personnel involved, served to guide those who came after them to change policies and techniques to improve outcomes.

I remained in the hospital for several weeks receiving IV fluids to prevent dehydration and malnutrition from the lack of appetite. Of course, wound care was at the top of the daily care regimen. Bandage changes were the most painful part of each day for me and tested the nerves of my parents. Mom and dad took turns accompanying me to wound care which meant listening to their little girl scream in pain!

Relatives and friends continued to come assist my parents by staying with me a few hours at a time allowing for some much needed rest and mental break from the situation. It was described as being like a revolving door of people who came to perform a relay by swapping me from person to person for walking duty which seemed to decrease my tears more than any other tactic. Various games and activities were used to distract me from the constant pain and discomfort.

Unfortunately, the extra special Christmas celebration in our new home would have to wait until the next year. Santa Claus visited me on December 25 in my hospital room where I was surrounded by family members who were grateful I was alive. I was discharged from the hospital a few days after Christmas just in time to ring in a new year. (Hopefully, 1965 would end better than 1964.)

I can't begin to imagine how my parents were able to cope during those long days in the hospital. It must have been brutal! Even when the hospital stay was over, the ordeal was not. The follow-up doctor visits and continued bandage changes served to prolong their mental torture. In the current medical environment, I would have been going to physical and occupational therapy for stretching exercises and pressure garment fitting in hopes of reducing any scarring and contractures. But, in 1964, no specialized care existed, at least in our area. Verbal instructions from the doctor and nurses were carried out at home by family. It was left to my mom to apply oils and massage my arm in attempts to kept me mobile and decrease the scar. As she administered my burn therapy, she was surely reliving the nightmare on a daily basis.

The wounds on my face and upper body were first and second degree burns that healed rapidly without any scarring. My right arm, however, was a deep burn that required extensive bandage changes and months of follow-up visits to a physician. When the wounds on the right arm healed a residual scar

stretching from just above the wrist to just below the
shoulder remained. The scar is a little lighter in color
than the surrounding skin with an uneven surface
and a wrinkled appearance. My outcome was one of
the most favorable because there are no problems
with motor function, sensation, joint motion, or pain.

CHAPTER 3

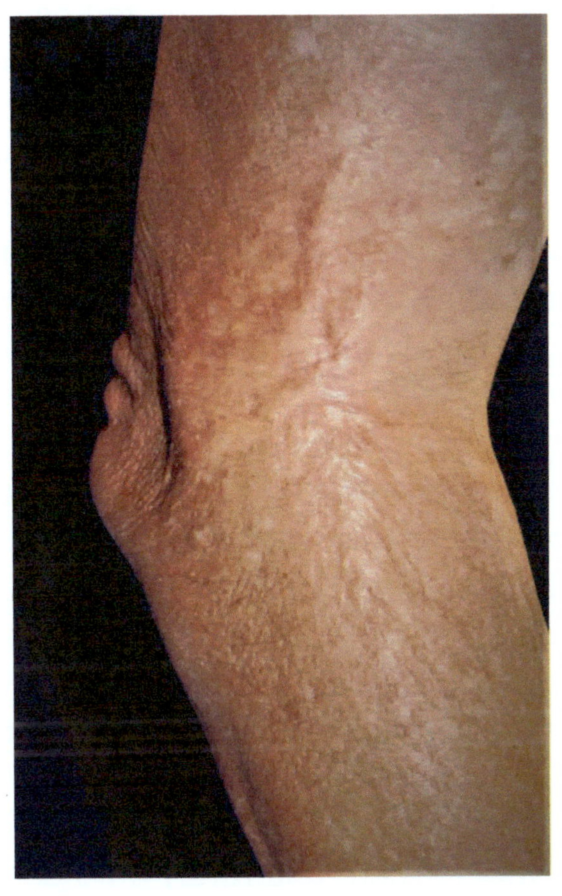

Adjusting To The View

From time to time my mother would use creative methods to conceal my scar. For many years a pair of portraits of myself and my sister, as small children about the same age, hung in our home. The photographer had taken a frontal picture of me wearing a short sleeve shirt. Because my scar was not visible in the photo, I assumed the picture had been taken before my accident. As we grew up, my parents replaced the photos with more current snapshots. The old photos were put away and forgotten until as an adult I was rummaging through some boxes and discovered them still in good condition. When I learned my age in the photo I knew it was taken after my accident. It was several more years before I got the courage to question my parents about the absence of my scar in the photo. Reluctantly, my parents admitted to having had an artist touch up the photo to cover my scar. This is the moment I began to realize how deeply their guilt and remorse remained hidden from me.

Even though I am a mature adult now, there are still times, in the presence of my parents, when I wear clothes that reveal my scar I can see in their faces the horror relived. I am thankful for no memory of this awful incident and rarely am I consciously aware of the scar. It has always been a part of me. It is me and part of who I am.

The psychological impact of forever being branded is devastating. My ability to adjust to living with a burn scar was enhanced by the fact that I have no recollection of my physical appearance before my scarring occurred. Because my parents coped with the tragedy by not talking about what happened actually helped me cope extremely well. My family did not discuss the incident, at least not around me. Therefore, the resulting scar was never an issue for me. However, occasionally I would ask a few general questions about that day. The generic answer was always something like, "You pulled a pot of boiling water over on your arm. The scar was created by the sweater you were wearing at the time. It was a few weeks before Christmas in 1964 and you spent several weeks in the hospital."

The details of the incident described earlier were revealed to me much later in life as an adult and at my insistence that I know what happened. As a physical therapist treating burn patients the subject of my burn would often arise. I wanted to be able to relate better to my patients by giving details.

In fact, it was not until later in life that I began to think about whether or not the situation under which I might be meeting someone for the first time would necessitate the need to inform them I have a scar on my right arm. For example, growing up in the deep south the temperature outside is warm enough most of the year to wear short sleeve shirts. This scenario created frequent opportunities for my scars to be exposed to everyone I might encounter.

Memories of being in public places, like a restaurant or the grocery store, and noticing people staring at me are reminders of how unaware I was about the visibility of my scar. When I found myself in such a situation, I would immediately think that maybe my zipper was unzipped or that I had food on my face, only to realize they were staring at my scar. I would actually be relieved to know they were looking at my scar instead of knowing I had committed some social faux pas!

Most strangers simply attempt to pretend they didn't notice my scars. Actually, my social skills improved as a result of others being uncomfortable with my appearance. I became better at making small talk to ease the tension and getting them to focus on another subject. I have never been someone who worried too much about what others thought of me. However, I never wanted to be inconsiderate of anyone's feelings or give the impression that I displayed my scar like some badge of honor.

Throughout my childhood I don't ever remember other kids being mean to me or making fun of me about my scar, at least not to my face. I have always felt comfortable in my skin. When sharing my story with others, especially other burn patients, I think they sense how comfortable I am with my appearance. Hopefully, they see a burn patient who has completed the wound healing process and has achieved pain free, normal movement over the burn area. There is life after being burned and it can be a happy and productive one.

My positive outlook about my scar and my good physical recovery has a lot to do with the great support system I had growing up. I was never made to feel different or treated special because of my scar. I was expected to do all the same chores and school work as others. Also, I was allowed to participate in most extracurricular activities that interested me.

Now, I don't want to mislead the readers into thinking that my life has been without incident regarding perceptions about my scar. My family and friends rarely restricted my activities or my exposure to certain situations as a result of my accident. However, a few circumstances would always bring out their apprehension.

When I became a teenager I wanted to learn to cook, a process that, in the south, required learning to brew tea. As you can imagine, just the thought of me getting around boiling water and/or brewing tea gave both parents and grandparents tremendous anxiety. So, they always managed to find a reason to keep me out of the kitchen when the meal preparation reached the point for use of the stove or oven. Usually, they would ask me to play the piano for them while they did the cooking and I would always oblige. One day I convinced my grandmother to let me help her with the actual cooking part of the dinner prep. From the time I put the pots on the stove burners she stood over me like a mother hen protecting her chick! I thought at any moment she was going to grab the pots out of my hand and finish the tasks herself. At the time, I thought her apprehension was because she did not think I had the ability to perform the tasks. As an adult looking back over the moment, I realize she was experiencing high anxiety over the possibility of another accident for which she would not be able to forgive herself if it were to happen again.

As a junior in high school I entered our local "America's Junior Miss Pageant" (now known as "Distinguished Young Women"). Contestants needed several outfits, including an evening gown. My mother and I shopped in area boutiques for some appropriate dresses. It was actually a wonderful bonding time with my mother. However, when I would try on sleeveless dresses I could see the distress written all over her face as she attempted to guide me towards dresses with some sleeve length to cover my scar. In fact, the dress I eventually bought was sleeveless. My mother and I both agreed that the dress looked good on me . At the time, I remember being confused that she sounded sincere about the dress looking good, but her face said something else entirely. Now, I realize that the "something else" was probably suppressed feelings about the accident that surfaced during times when the physical scars might be exposed to the world. When I participated in a competitive activity I did so with the expectation that I would be judged as the other contestants and not given any special consideration because of my scar.

Thinking back, I'm not sure why I was never self-conscious about my scar.   During my adolescent years I obsessed about the same things any teenage girl would - appearance. I always worried about my weight, hair style, make-up, and, of course, boys. But, never about the presence of the scar on my right arm. I am thankful that I could remove worries about something I could do nothing about and concentrate on some of the controllable factors.

In general, people are timid about approaching others who are different physically, especially about asking the details of how and why someone is not like them. In fact, people are often reluctant to even acknowledge that they notice the differences. These reactions and feelings are normal and understandable because everyone handles their life events differently. It would be difficult to know who might be open to discussion or who might be offended.

My most memorable moment with strangers came during a post-graduate physical therapy continuing education course. At most of these courses there is a practical portion which requires the participants to practice some of the treatment techniques learned in the course. This particular course was about shoulder treatments, so, during the practical lab portion, we were going to have to remove our shirts to expose bare shoulders and arms (women wore sports bras). When the time came for the practical portion of the course the instructor divided the class into small groups. For my turn as the patient, I removed my long sleeve t-shirt to expose the shoulder area. A look of surprise appeared on the faces of most of the other participants. My initial thought was whether or not I was having some sort of clothing malfunction. After a few seconds had passed they all suddenly looked away in embarrassment as I realized it was my scar they were so politely trying to ignore. I apologized for the shock and gave the brief version of events that caused my scar reminding them that I don't remember any of the events due to my young age at the time of the accident. All classmates seemed to continue with the course without further distraction.

I thought about this incident for weeks afterwards. I knew I had to be more sensitive about preparing others to see my scar for the first time. If "professionals" would react to my scar in such a manner, then how could I have expected others to handle "the viewing" any differently?

CHAPTER 4

Personal

vs

Professional

My high school, like most high schools across America, hosted a career day once a year for the juniors and seniors. Professionals from different career fields would come speak to the students about the specifics of their job duties as well as the training and educational requirements. During these sessions the students were given printed materials about each job for review and comparison later. Among these brochures was one about the various healthcare professions offered at The University of South Alabama with a detailed description of each specialty. Within the pages of this brochure I read for the first time about Physical Therapy. Both the job duties and the wide range of possible work environments made physical therapy sound like an interesting and challenging career.

After completing my prerequisites, I was accepted into the physical therapy program at our local university.   Like most professional programs the study load was heavy! Toward the end of the program when most of the classroom portion of the educational process has been completed, the internship portion (on the job training) begins. One aspect of the internship is to introduce the students to as many real life situations as possible. The hope is that these experiences will give the students some depth of practical knowledge to reference when they encounter similar scenarios once they are licensed, practicing professionals.

The portions of the curriculum taught in the classrooms and actually used in professional practices depends upon post-graduation employment venues. My 20+ years (and counting) in health care began as an acute care physical therapist (practicing in a hospital setting treating inpatients). The acute care environment attracts professionals who enjoy the adrenaline rush of fast paced treatment schedules and quick progression of care.   Every work day is challenging, stressful, educational, rewarding, and interesting!

At the University of South Alabama Medical Center where I worked as a staff physical therapist, I was exposed to the true meaning of generalized physical therapy practice. This facility was designated the level one trauma center for our region, complete with a burn unit.   In addition to the multiple trauma victims, I was hired by the university hospital with the understanding that I would be trained to treat burn victims, a career move my parents failed to comprehend given my own brush with death as a child.

The initial six months of training was intense and rigorous. The training included learning splint fabrication, additional wound care procedures, and stretching techniques specific to burn care. Patient care in the burn center required me to utilize almost every aspect of my classroom knowledge – anatomy, neurology, physiology, pharmacology, psychology,…

well you get the idea. It was like being in school all over again.

All ages and socioeconomic groups can potentially be burn victims. Children present a unique set of issues because of their varying levels of understanding of the situation around their injuries and the treatment techniques used to care for them. Also, the parents and family members of these younger patients play an important part in the healing process by giving the patient a familiar presence in an unfamiliar environment.

All healthcare workers have stories about certain patients who have touched their hearts and left lasting impressions upon everyone involved in the care. One of my stories involves a girl who was burned in a similar manner and around the same age as myself. My encounter with this child would have a profound affect on how I would come to view the direction of my career as a physical therapist, especially when dealing with burn patients.

On this particular day, I was working in the wound care area of the physical therapy department which meant changing the bandages of all types of wounds, including burns of patients not in the burn unit. (Once a patient is transferred out of the burn unit and into a regular room, the bandages are changed in the wound care area of the physical therapy department.) I had been briefed by the burn team physical therapist on the specifics of both the bandage change and treatment to be performed on the burn patients I would be handling. There was child, a young girl, on my list who was scheduled for a relatively routine type of bandage change and treatment regimen for her level of injury. But, treating a child is rarely routine and can be unnerving regardless of the circumstances.

The hospital had a central transport system that handled all patient travel between the different departments. Like most of the burn patients, the child was transported to the physical therapy department via stretcher. Having been to the physical therapy department several times already this little girl was aware of what was going to be done. So, as soon as the transporter turned the stretcher into our department she began crying.   Per hospital protocol, a family member is allowed in the treatment area with children. This policy is especially helpful when children are undergoing a painful procedure. That day, her father was present during the treatment session.

Following treatment procedure protocol, I donned the required wound care garments: (1) a long sleeve, knee-length paper gown that had Velcro closures in the back and elastic wrist bands, (2) a paper mask over my nose and mouth that had elastic ear loops, (3) a paper hair net with elastic band to secure it around my head, and (4) rubber gloves. As I entered the treatment area the decibel level of her crying went to ear drum piercing! (I'm sure to the child these therapy sessions seemed like "aliens coming to "visit" when we entered dressed in these protective garments.)

After reciting my usual reassurance to the child that it won't hurt much and the procedure will be over soon, I worked as carefully and as quickly as I could to remove the old bandages and cleanse the wounds in preparation for new bandages. The bandage change procedure itself was not extremely painful and the child had been given the usual pain medication. Children often cry more from fear than from any accompanying pain.

With tears streaming down his face, her father was dutifully assisting me by holding his daughter and attempting to keep her still while trying to comfort her. Having parents present while performing such painful procedures can be tricky, but I believe that it is an important part of the healing process for everyone involved. He was a kind and gentle man who expressed love for his daughter and respect for our team. He frequently thanked us for the compassionate care we gave his daughter. Even though it was an accident, he often voiced guilt about the situation surrounding how she was burned.

By the time I had applied the new bandages over the wounds I was sweating bullets. I stepped back and removed the long sleeve gown and mask. At last I could move in comfort with my short sleeve scrubs, no mask, and no gloves. Almost as if cued by some director from behind the curtain, the little girl stopped crying! (Usually, the children do not stop crying until they leave the department.) I paused for a few seconds in panic thinking something was wrong. Her father looked at me in shock! His daughter was looking at my right arm with her head tilted to one side in bewilderment. The removal of my gown had revealed the scar on my right arm. She reached out with her hand and gently touched my scar followed by a few soft strokes over my scar. Then, she looked up into my eyes and with the most kind, caring voice asked, "Hurt?" I was speechless, frozen with my jaw open. I had no idea how dramatic it would be for a burn patient to see my scar. Barely maintaining my composure I briefly told both patient and parent how I had been burned in a very similar manner. I explained to her father that because the accident occurred at such a young age she would probably, like myself, not remember any of the pain and suffering she was experiencing. My heart was filled with joy to see the look on her father's face become one of relief.

From that day forward I had a new sense of purpose for being a part of the burn team. I felt my career was headed in the right direction and that truly, one person can make a difference. Until this encounter I believed it was important to separate personal and professional lives. However, my personal life experiences could clearly have an impact on my professional outcomes.

In that moment I began to understand what my parents had endured some 25 years earlier. In the coming months and years that I worked with burn victims I gained not only invaluable professional knowledge and skills, but insight into the psychological effects my entire incident had on my parents.

The professional and personal aspects of my life continued to cross paths.

CHAPTER 5

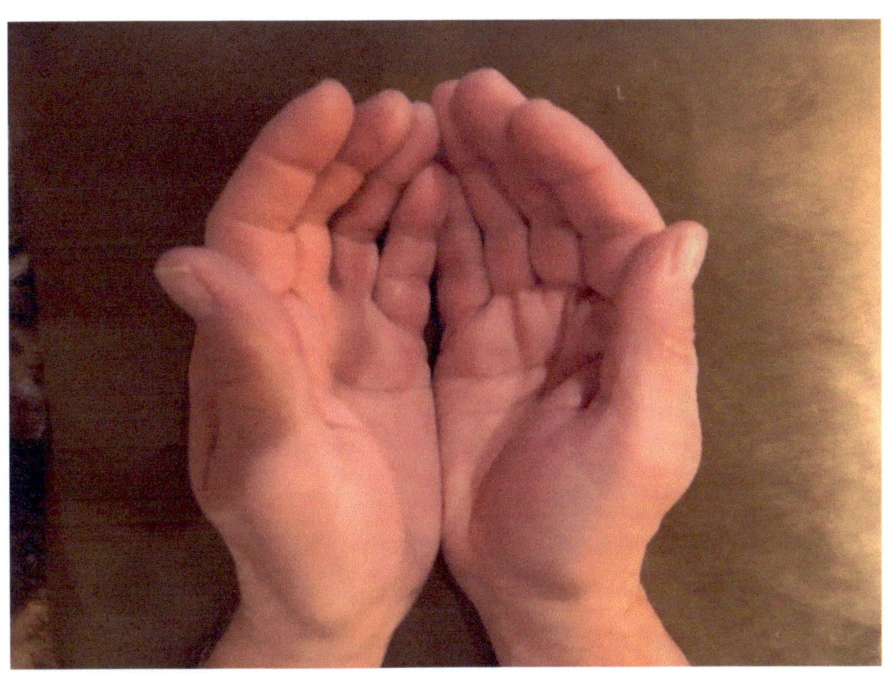

Sharing

Treatment sessions similar to the one I had with the 16 month old burn child were not common occurrences, but since that encounter I was less hesitant to share my story. Sharing the similarities and differences of an injury with someone who has survived the same kind of trauma provides comfort and hope to the soul.   However, thinking someone would be interested in hearing the chain of events that caused my accident would be presumptuous. Being perceived as a therapist who thought she knew how every burn patient felt was never my intention.

Every injury has a unique situation and set of circumstances. So, each patient adjusts to their "loss of self" differently. The adjustment time frames are dependent on the severity of their burns and what type of other injuries may accompany the burns. For example, broken bones or a head injury. While treating patients in the burn unit I witnessed many instances when the patients would verbally lash out at the staff in understandable moments of anger and despair.   Mostly, they were expressing how misunderstood they felt. Sharing my story with patients under such circumstances might seem like the most opportune time, but it could make them feel like we were marginalizing their feelings. Often, I waited until they were transferred out of the burn unit before I revealed my scar.   The protective garments required in the burn unit when entering a patient's room made it easy to hide my scar.

Once a patient was transferred out of the burn unit and placed in a regular room they would begin coming down to the therapy department for treatment. Without the protective garments required in the burn unit, my scar was discreetly visible when I wore a short sleeve shirt.   The first glance at my scar by a patient usually sparked a candid and productive conversation about what kind of recovery time and quality of life they could expect. Throughout the course of their stay at our facility I might have several conversations with them about these matters. I was willing to talk to them as many times as necessary in order to help them get back to living life.

The conversations with patients included the physiological process that the body goes through both when being burned and healing the wounds. Understanding the procedures we are using, why they are being performed and at least an estimated time frame for recovery would help the mental process of dealing with the pain and discomfort. Skin is our barrier to the outside world which protects our internal structures. Even after the wounds are closed they are still in a healing mode. The fragile skin continues to need some protection. The deeper the burn the more complicated the process because skin graft surgeries are necessary.

Deep, full thickness burns can result in raised scarring because of subcutaneous skin damage. As subcutaneous skin heals without the full thickness of the outer skin it exerts a pressure greater that the fragile new outer skin can tolerate. Therefore, a raised scar can develop. Patients with deep burns are fitted for a pressure garment to wear over that part of the body. Pressure garments assist the fragile skin in maintaining skin integrity during the healing process. The garments are custom made and can be ordered in many different colors to blend with clothing thus increasing patient compliance with wearing them. Pressure garments for the facial area are difficult to fit and, as you might imagine, uncomfortable to wear. Facial burns are particularly damaging to the body image of a patient and require multiple surgeries when reconstruction of ears, noses, lips, and even eyelids are necessary. More surgery means extending the recovery time and prolonging the adjustment time to the "new self." Socially, these patients usually retreat to the confines of their homes until the scars are mostly healed and the garments are no longer required, or when they think "the view" is better.

Pressure garments were developed several years after I was burned. Fortunately, I do not have a raised scar. However, my parents consulted a plastic surgeon as my wounds were healing in an attempt to eliminate my scar. The recommendation was to wait until I was around 15 years old to see how much I would "grow into the scar." As advised, we consulted a plastic surgeon when I was a teenager. The surgeon informed us that the skin grafts would cover only the prominent portion of the scar and would create yet another scar in the area of the body where the skin would be harvested. I did not want to create another scar to only partially cover-up the old one. Plus, the surgery would take up part of my summer vacation! My parents left the decision up to me.

My decision to decline the surgery was met with disappointment by my parents, but they did not try to change my mind. I have not regretted the choice. By this time in all our lives I think we had accepted the situation and were thankful that the outcome was positive. Leaving the scar in place has allowed me to bring hope to those with whom I share my story.

Discharge from the hospital did not necessarily mean going home.   Patients that are medically stable, but not yet capable of caring for themselves independently at home need additional treatment.   An inpatient rehab hospital treats patients in the subacute phase of their recovery.   Patients with severe burns often require at least a short stay in this type of facility. While employed at such a rehab center in central Georgia, we admitted a few burn patients in need of a little extra adjustment time.

The other professionals at the facility were aware of my burn care experience, so, from time to time they would get my input on the treatment of a burn patient. One of these patients was a man with second and third degree burns to his legs. His case was complicated by other serious injuries making it necessary for him to receive extensive inpatient rehab. I was familiar with his situation because I had performed some treatment sessions with him during a few of my weekend rotations. He was a stocky, middle-aged man who had a very supportive family. He was diligent with the performance of his therapy regimen, but frustrated at what he perceived as a slow pace of healing. The movement in his legs continued to be painful and pain medication was still necessary for him to tolerate the bandage changes.

A few days before he was scheduled to be discharged home with his family I assisted the treating therapist with some of the home instruction to him and his wife. During the conference he appeared to be emotional and actually began to get tears in his eyes. Just discussing the impending discharge and the adjustments that would need to be made at home caused anxiety and concern. He was obviously embarrassed by his show of emotion as his wife tried to assure him the changes would be fine. I explained to both him and his wife that these feelings were completely normal. Patients become comfortable in the rehab environment and, as discharge approaches, fear of leaving the trained staff that has cared for them and made them feel safe, increases.

Upon returning home, he would need to give himself and his family some time to adjust to his presence.

After calming his nerves about his readiness for discharge, I could see he still had some doubt. He had lingering questions like how or when the pain in his legs would subside, especially with movement. Like most inpatient rehab patients, he had envisioned being completely back to his pre-accident status before returning home. Therefore, the need for any assistance at home was both humbling and disappointing. Not to mention he still had some bandages on his legs which meant not knowing what the final scarring would look like.

Cautiously, I decided to proceed with sharing my story with him in an effort relieve a little of his apprehension going into the next stage of his healing process. I rolled up the right sleeve of my shirt to show him my right arm scar and briefly told him how I was burned. He had a surprised yet curious look on his face. After demonstrating the normal, pain free motion of my right arm he seemed to be able to focus more on retaining the home instructions. Still, I wasn't sure exactly how my story had affected him.

On the morning of his discharge, he and his wife came by the physical therapy department to thank me for sharing my story with them. He said he wanted me to realize how much it helped just hearing from another burn victim that life will eventually return to normal. He and his family thought

all the doctors, nurses, and therapists were extremely knowledgeable, kind, and professional. However,
hearing from the voice of experience was a valuable
adjunct to the program.

CHAPTER 6

A Prodigy

As I stated in Chapter three, children present a unique set of issues including varying levels of understanding about the treatment procedures being utilized for their healing. In rare instances, the intellect of the child equals or surpasses that of the professionals. One of the most difficult cases for me psychologically involved a 12-year-old boy who possessed such an intellect .

By all appearances, this boy was from a stable family with parents who stayed informed about every aspect of his life. His father had a military background which probably accounted for the family's rigid rules for both schoolwork and recreational activities. The parents attempted to raise a disciplined and well-behaved young man by imposing strict rules and high expectations for both him and his younger brother. Part of their strategy meant summer projects every year for both the children. These projects were meant to be thought-provoking, but they also hoped to enable the boys to develop additional skills.

During this particular summer, my patient's project had proven extremely challenging and he became aware he may not meet the deadline set for him by his father. Knowing his dad would not tolerate any excuses, he became distraught over the possibility of disappointing his parents. He decided the only way to ensure a passing grade by his father was to become physically unable to perform the task; Or, worse, he considered being alive was an embarrassment to his family. (These are thoughts the patient shared with our team throughout the course of his treatment.)

This intelligent boy devised a plan that would cause the whole family great mental agony. It would also cause him great physical pain.

On his scheduled day to perform yard work at his home, the patient went out to the shed in the back yard to retrieve equipment and supplies. At first, the family heard the usual sounds of the lawn mower and could see him from the window as he stopped to collect the grass clippings. Then, a longer than usual break time occurred and the parents became concerned. The younger brother was sent out into the yard to find out what assistance, if any, his brother might need. What the younger brother was about discover could not have been imagined by his family.

As the young one turned the corner to the shed, he found his older brother sitting in their family's wheelbarrow. This seemed like an odd way to take a break. As the young one walked closer, to his horror, he realized his older brother was sitting in a pool of gasoline! His brother's entire body was covered in gasoline! In his brother's hand was a match ready to strike!

The younger brother frantically ran toward him yelling "don't do it!" The young one managed to tackle him to the ground, knocking him out of the wheelbarrow and onto the grass. After a brief wrestling match on the ground, the older brother overpowered and broke free from the young one's grip. The young one continued to scream "you don't have to do this" while the older one responded with "I'm a failure." The young one continued his pleas, stating he would help with the project and no one would need to know. (Obviously, the young one understood the dilemma facing his brother.) The older one was not convinced and he lit the match!

Hearing the commotion outside, the parents went to investigate. Expecting to find the usual sibling argument, they rounded the corner of the shed just in time to see their son light up like a torch! Both shock and panic filled their bodies for the first few moments before they began acting swiftly. Fortunately, they were able to extinguish the flames quickly, but the young man's burns were still severe. They rushed him to the ER for treatment of face, arm, hand, and body burns.

After he was admitted to our burn unit and all the medical professionals had performed their assessments, the team discussed his case in conference. As per protocol, Social Services and Child Protective Services would do their investigations. They determined he had overbearing parents with sometimes unrealistic expectations of their children, but ruled that this was not abusive situation. The inability of the older boy to attain some of these goals had manifested in the most extreme of behaviors in order to avoid disappointing his parents. It was now our mission as a team to heal both his physical wounds and his psychological scars.

As a therapist, I had to be aware of all aspects of the patient's condition which might affect his treatment outcome. The child's strict parents made getting him to cooperate with the therapy regimen relatively easy. So, compliance was never an issue! However, he was a challenge intellectually for all team members. He asked questions about every detail of his care. He demonstrated a knowledge about chemistry and biology that was well beyond his years!

One day I was assisting another therapist in adjusting his hand splints. We were having trouble getting the hooks for the rubber bands to stick to his fingertips (dynamic splints use rubber bands as resistance against the constant pull of healing scar tissue.) In a matter of fact way, he looked at us and said we needed a glue that had polymers compatible with the hook and nail molecules. Because of his intelligence, he could have been condescending with his suggestions and criticisms; But, he was respectful and polite with all of his comments.

He progressed rapidly with all aspects of his healing process probably because of his disciplined background. It was a shame that these same characteristics brought about the circumstances for him to be in our facility. I have been unable to reconcile how such an intelligent young man could see any benefit from setting himself on fire. How could it solve any issues? Maybe it made his parents relax some of their requirements, or, at least rethink their approach so that he and his brother could grow into well adjusted young men. My hope is that he went on to use his intellect to continue obtaining knowledge he could ultimately use to help make this world a better place.

CHAPTER 7

Domestic

Violence

Childish behavior sometimes continues into adulthood. For centuries, adults have inflicted pain and suffering onto persons they supposedly love and care about. Whether resulting from an act of jealous rage or a fit of anger, the results can be just as life-altering. In some cases, attempting to defend ourselves against these acts of violence does not end well for all involved. One couple found themselves explaining how an argument got so out of hand that they both wound up being admitted to the hospital with third degree burns.

Upon investigation, Social Services found that the husband would come home from work in the evenings after making a pit stop at one of the local bars. Of course, this meant probably a little too much alcoholic beverage had been consumed. Alcohol consumption affects people differently. In his case, it turned her loving husband into a violent tyrant. On this particular occasion, alcohol contributed to a devastating outcome.

As soon as the husband entered the house, he started his usual complaining about things that might seem trivial to a sober person. On this particular evening, he was dissatisfied with dinner. I'm not sure if he didn't like what she was cooking for dinner or that it simply wasn't ready at the precise time he wanted to eat. Whatever lit his fuse, he came at her with all his strength while she was still preparing the meal. A push and a shove, then a slap, evolved into swinging fists. All the while, the husband screamed threats on his wife's life and shouted demeaning comments. She could not take it anymore! Reaching for the nearest object to use as a defense weapon, she grabbed the handle of the grease-filled frying pan and swung it at him. The hot grease hit his chest and face and splattered onto his arms. He dropped to his knees in pain! Unfortunately, she failed to release the pan before some of the grease splashed back on her face and chest as well. Now, they both had serious burns which needed medical attention.

Fortunately, the neighbors had the good sense to call the police. Authorities arrived to find the husband still in a homocidal rant which continued as he was loaded into the ambulance. The local authorities, who had made multiple visits to their residence for domestic disputes, were familiar with this couple. This incident was much more horrifying than usual. Both husband and wife had to be taken to the same hospital due the seriousness of their injuries. They required the expertise that could only be found at our facility.

Throughout their stay at our facility, they were separated because the husband constantly verbalized his desire to harm his wife, vowing revenge when he got the opportunity. As a woman providing his care, I never felt comfortable in his presence. On a few occasions, he made statements to me that were obviously intended to intimidate me, even though they were not direct threats. For example, he would say things like "what kind of people keep a man from seeing his wife" and "what would you expect me to do to someone who has burned me." I got the feeling he kept his temper in check so that we would continue to treat him. But, I also felt he had every intention of executing revenge after he was discharged.

I could not imagine why someone would want to stay with another person who did not want them. Why waste energy beating them and risking jail? My grandma always said there are plenty of fish in the sea. Just cast your line on another shore.

CHAPTER 8

John Doe

Occasionally, we as physical therapists are not told all the details about how a patient was burned. Some circumstances were stranger than others. Because I am a big fan of mystery and crime solving television shows, it is not surprising that one case in particular has remained in my memory banks.

I arrived on the burn unit later than I would usually report for duty because the regular therapist was out sick for the day. As I rushed through the double doors, I noticed a patient sitting up in his bedside chair quite calmly. Something about his stare caught my attention and I paused for a brief look to make sure he was not in distress. His breakfast tray was untouched and his lethargy concerned me. The pain medicine and the severity of his burns could have caused his loss of appetite. After I observed for a few minutes, I was satisfied he was stable for the moment. So, I continued to the conference room where I would receive a briefing from the team on all the patients.

John Doe, as this man was designated because he was found alone and without identification, was admitted the day before. An anonymous caller had dialed 911 to report this man sitting, tied to a chair in a warehouse. He appeared to be badly burned. Police and fire department personnel responded to discover he had been doused in gasoline and set fire and apparently left for dead. He was subsequently flown to our facility for treatment. His face was burned too badly for photo identification. His lungs

were so damaged he could not speak. The top layer
of skin was burned off of his fingers preventing fin-
gerprint identification. Also, his sight was diminished
from the injury.

During the week following his admission, he
was cooperative with his treatment plan, but never
revealed any additional details about the incident.
No one came forward to identify him. Theories and
speculation among the staff were constantly evolv-
ing. Possibilities of the cause of his burns ranged
from a jealous boyfriend or spouse to a gang war.
His recovery seemed to be progressing normally for
the severity of his injuries.

On about day seven or eight of his stay, according to nursing staff, a male visitor appeared one
morning during breakfast. The man only stayed
about 15 minutes and left before any other staff
member had chance to speak with him or even get a
good look at him. (Breakfast can be a busy time on
the unit depending on how many patients need assistance eating.) Tragically, John Doe died about 30
minutes after the mysterious visitor exited the room.

This happened before all the strict rules for patient privacy and accurate visitor logs had been put
into place. Officially, he died of complications from
his injuries and no connection to the visitor was sug-
gested. However, neither John Doe nor his visitor
were ever identified.

I can't imagine what would make me want to
burn another living being alive. I have never suffered

such an injustice. I suppose if someone had done such a thing to a family member or close friend I would consider returning the favor. However, having heard the screams and moans of burn victims, I'm not sure I could actually light the match. The difficult treatment sessions are hard enough on my psyche, even though I know I am helping patients recover. What that burden would feel like, knowing I had caused such anguish, might be too much for me.

CHAPTER 9

Construction
Explosion

Burns that affect a majority of the body's surface, especially when the face and hands are involved, can be extremely gruesome. The treatment approach has to be a detailed, methodical regimen. Any variance from the planned protocol can mean a less than favorable outcome. When a burn victim suffers such a major trauma, the recovery can be complicated by guilt, either on the part of the patient and/or other people involved. The stress level goes up a notch when a workplace accident occurs, especially when the events take place at a high profile construction site. For a young therapist, like myself at the time, it can be quite the learning experience with both the treatment techniques and the logistics of the team approach.

One night after work, I sat down on my couch to watch the evening news. To my dismay, I saw a story about an explosion at a commercial construction site in our area. Evidently, the accident resulted in one fatality and one man hospitalized in critical condition at our facility! My mind began to race with anticipation and anxiety because the limited information I heard on television caused me a sleepless night thinking about what the next days and weeks would be like for our burn team.

During our morning team conference, we learned this patient's condition was very serious with burns that were both electrical and heat-related. The patient had suffered electrical burns on both hands, and the explosion had caused severe burns over a majority of his body.   The types of burns and percentage of the body burned would make his treatment timeframe extremely long and complicated. His hand burns alone presented challenges for our team that would test the cohesiveness of our approach. Our permanent team members had a solid grasp of the necessity for the coordination of every detail in the treatment regimen. Every team member played a vital role in the patient's successful treatment outcome. The residents and interns that worked under our attending physician often depended on us to guide them through the unusual protocols that exist in such an environment. However, once in a while a rogue resident can put the entire process in jeopardy.

This patient had electrical burns that were so severe that the surgeons had to remove some of his fingertips. The fire burns destroyed so much skin that multiple grafts were required on the remainder of his fingers and hands. This set in motion our splinting protocol, which assists in maintaining joint mobility by preventing excessive scar tissue formation. At the time, part of the protocol was for the splints to be worn 24 hours a day, except during dressing changes. Splints could also be removed for short periods every few hours as a comfort measure if the patient needed relief from the constant pull, but medication could not remove all pain sensations associated with burn care.

After several of these procedures, the patient himself became familiar with the protocol increasing compliance. Surgeons were hoping that one last procedure would restore his hands. This delicate and intricate procedure required advanced skills on the part of the surgeons, therefore, advanced therapy knowledge was needed to ensure proper follow-up treatment. Part of the followup was the splint application wear time.   All staff were aware of a splint protocol even though they might not be familiar with the details. So, as usual, we left explicit, written instructions for the staff about the specifics of the splint protocol.

Bandages are not generally removed after surgery for three days unless the cultures performed during surgery begin to grow bacteria and the risk for infection warrants removing and replacing the dressings. Fortunately, cultures had grown out normal and the bandages (including the splints) were scheduled to be removed on the fourth day after surgery.

On the first morning his dressings were scheduled to be removed, I arrived a few minutes early on the burn unit. I talked with the team about coordinating the dressing change with his therapy session, which would include splint assessment. To my surprise, I found the splints had already been removed the night before and never reapplied. The splints had been off for approximately 8-10 hours! According to the nurse, the doctors decided to perform the initial dressing change on the evening shift, but neglected to reapply the splints or write the usual orders for 24-hour splint application as per our protocol. I contacted the resident on call reiterating the importance of our splinting protocol and requested the necessary order for splint application. Also, I informed the nurse about the conversation I had with the resident.

Most of the patient's therapy session was spent stretching his hands in order to regain the lost range of motion caused by the splints not being reapplied. I discussed with the nurse the importance of following protocol and having therapy present during that time. The amount of time the patient needed additional pain medication would decrease the agony of therapy procedures. The nurse assured me she would pass this information along to the next shift. As with all therapy treatments performed, documentation of all communication with other health professionals and the actions taken were written in the chart.

The next morning, I arrived expecting to coordinate a dressing change and therapy session with the nursing staff. Combining the two procedures makes it easier for the patient to have stretching and splint assessment performed at the same time so the bandages are removed less frequently. I was informed the doctors had once again performed another late shift dressing change and the hand splints were applied per the protocol. However, according to the nurse, the patient began to complain that the splints were too tight and requested the strapping be loosened. The nurse stated she informed the resident on call. The resident ordered the splints removed for patient comfort. No reapply order was written. So, splints had been off the patient again for about 8-10 hours.

My frustration was visible because I could not understand what would make the resident write an order that could have such detrimental consequences for the functional outcome of the patient. Also, I could not understand why the nurses would not take more initiative to remind the residents about such an important detail in our protocol! Again, I called the resident to reemphasize the importance of proper splinting for positive outcomes. He stated his understanding of the necessity to follow protocol and wrote the required order.

I spent another long treatment session attempting to regain the lost hand and finger range of motion for the patient. Unfortunately, I could not achieve the same motion that was lost, but it was close enough for hope that the next few days of stretching and splinting would get his motion back to baseline. Therefore, I had to adjust the splints to accommodate the lost motion. The patient was very grateful for my attention to detail and stated he would be more proactive about the splints after future dressing changes. All of these facts were documented in the chart at the end of the treatment sessions.

When I arrived on the burn unit the following day, I felt confident that my communication and education of the burn team had been sufficient to assume they would adhere to the protocol. What I discovered changed my entire outlook about our process and caused me to question my willingness to be a part of this team.

Upon entering the burn unit, I noticed the attending physician was in what appeared to be a very serious conference with his residents and interns. The attending did not seem pleased with whatever had occurred. As I passed the nursing station he called me over to the group. He asked if I was the therapist who had been treating the electrical burn patient. I confirmed I had been involved in the case for the last week. He promptly motioned for me to follow them into the dressing change room where the patient was waiting for his wounds to be re-wrapped. The attending physician immediately started interrogating me about the splinting technique and application protocol that was being used. As he continued, I was informed his hands were becoming contracted and whatever technique I had implemented was obviously not working. When he finished his rant, I realized I had been blamed for the entire situation - the failure of the surgery.

I soon learned my job and reputation were on the line because my boss came walking through the door! She was just in time to hear me recount the events of the last several days to the attending physician. You could have heard a pin drop when I finished telling my version and you could see the shocked look on everyone's face when I informed them everything was documented in the chart. The attending wanted to know immediately which residents had acted independently of the protocol - information I was more than willing to relate to him because he seemed more than glad to falsely accuse me of incompetence.

While my boss and the attending physician reviewed the chart, I went down to the therapy department to gather my thoughts and decide what to do. I was really uncertain I ever wanted to return to the unit to work with others who would do such an underhanded thing to their team member, not to mention how they had jeopardized the care of the patient.

Later that day, I got an apology from the team. The attending physician made it mandatory for him to get a call personally whenever a resident wrote an order contradictory to the protocol of the unit. The surgeon took the patient back into surgery and was able to regain the lost range of motion in his hands. Therapy protocol was rarely questioned after this incident.

The circumstances surrounding this case changed my perspective on the role health care workers play on a team approach to patient care.

The team must not only be familiar with the protocols and techniques involved in the treatment of patients, but also willing to support the team members attempting to implement these procedures. At times, this might mean questioning the decisions of those in authority who might not be as informed about the details of a particular case. Also, persons in authority should be open to suggestions from those actually performing the daily care. These professionals might have a clearer understanding of the overall goals of the treatments. This case highlights the humanity of all healthcare workers to get caught up on the hierarchy of the medical team rather than remaining focused on the goal of healing the patients.

On the days I was attempting to make sure the patient received the proper splinting for his hands, I was not thinking about being a rebel or trying to prove I was right. I simply wanted the best outcome for the patient. I was willing to use every resource at my disposal to try to ensure that he regained as much function as possible. In hindsight, I reflect on how my life as a burn survivor was coming full circle. My actions of simply doing my job caused positive change in the team dynamics. This process proved different from my journey years earlier, when my parents sought proper care, but got incompetence and neglect. Thankfully, my mother had the persistence to seek out another facility to make sure I was cared for properly.

In any situation that requires making choices, the right choice is not always the easy one. In fact, doing the right thing could be the most difficult choice. Each choice will have consequences. Choosing to do nothing will have the most detrimental consequence of all! We will not regret the things we have attempted and failed, we will regret the things we never attempted. Those people that are on the receiving end of your assistance and passion will always be grateful for your efforts and remember your kindness. My hope is that whatever kindness you have experienced you pay it forward.

FINAL THOUGHTS

My mother still has what remains of a Christmas arrangement that was sent by some friends while I was in the hospital. Over the years the arrangement became ragged and shabby. I asked mom many times why she didn't throw it away. She simply responded, "It has sentimental value."

Although the memories of that Christmas were extremely painful, I think the arrangement reminded her of the many family and friends that stood by them in such a dark hour of need. To my knowledge, the Christmas arrangement was the only memorabilia that my mother kept from that horrible incident. However, one painful reminder would always remain with us all - the scar on my right arm. The scar is the reason you are reading this book and I thank you.

Fortunately, because of my young age, I don't remember any of these events. But, this also means I don't remember any of the kind people who assisted my family.   So, whoever you are I am thankful for your time and effort. Whether you visited me in the hospital or helped after I went home, may God bless you.

ABOUT THE AUTHOR

Elizabeth Grey brings personal experience to her physical therapy practice by sharing her childhood accident with patients who need some extra encouragement during recovery. Her story is inspiring to anyone trying to get on with life after a tragic event.